S0-DUI-236

CONTENTS

THIS BUSINESS OF TELEVISION

Everyone watches television. It's the number one pastime in America. The average person in this country takes in four or five hours of television a day. TV is an important means of communication.

When TV began, there were only a handful of channels. Most of the airtime was filled with news, comedy-variety shows and dramas. People didn't have a lot of choice about what to watch. But now there's a whole universe at the end of your remote control!

You can still see news, dramas and variety shows on TV. But now there are other programs to choose from: sitcoms, movies, game shows, how-to shows, soap operas, court cases, concerts, sports—even shows that let you shop at home. Experimental programs help you find a new house or a new date. People can even broadcast shows from their basements. And, of course, commercials help pay for most of the shows we get to see.

With this huge variety of shows on TV comes a huge variety of TV jobs. Millions of people work behind the scenes to get these shows on the air. And with the television business growing at breakneck speed, there will always be a need for skilled and hardworking people.

You don't need four years of college to get TV skills. A lot of jobs, especially those that don't leave you sitting behind a desk, can be learned through experience. These are the kind of jobs we want to tell you about. If you're willing to work hard, you can start with your bare hands, sharp mind and good attitude. And you stand a good chance of succeeding.

If you're a young woman, you should know that there are a lot more guys in TV than there are women. But don't let that stop you.

The television industry employs people for a variety of jobs.

If you're a tough worker and have skills to offer, you can get hired. And every time a woman does a good job, she helps open doors for other women looking for similar work in the future.

In this book you'll meet some people who have found TV jobs that make them happy and proud. Listen to them—their advice, their stories and their insights. Try to imagine a day in their work shoes. Then look at yourself and figure out what your strengths are, what interests you have and what skills you want. Set some goals for yourself and read on. We'll help you get there.

PRODUCTION ASSISTANT

Nuts and Bolts of the Job

You're about to bite into your cheeseburger deluxe when a young woman in jeans hurries into the restaurant. You're not really sure why you notice her. She looks like a lot of people you know. But then she places her order—8 cheeseburgers, 6 special chicken sandwiches, 4 bacon cheeseburgers, 5 burgers deluxe, 12 large fries and 16 drinks! Why is this young woman ordering enough food to feed an army?

Production assistants like Michele offer general help for all parts of television production. Michele's job, she says, is "to take care of all the tedious tasks to free up the **producer**'s creativity and the crew's time."

A production assistant, or PA, can be asked to do "anything and everything." Michele's tasks range from going out to get a last-minute prop to paying bills to organizing crowd control to getting people—sometimes famous people—lunch. "None of these tasks are hard in and of themselves," Michele says. "It's a matter of getting them done quickly and under pressure."

When bosses give orders, they usually just say what they need—not how to accomplish it. PAs have to solve the "how" on their own. Requests like "Find me a lava lamp" or "Get all those people to be quiet and stand back" are much easier said than done. A good production assistant is resourceful and flexible and is able to find a solution—fast.

Michele likes to arrive at work early. It gives her time to settle in and make her list of things to do. "If I have tasks that carried over from the day before, I do them right away," she explains. "Then I

Handling phone calls is just one task a PA performs.

meet with my boss and she tells me what needs to be done that day."

A typical workday for Michele can include almost anything. Her boss might ask her to log tapes. That means to watch videotapes and write down what happens and what's said. The tape log helps producers and editors find the good parts of a videotape quickly. Michele might also be asked to dub tapes—to make videotape copies.

If Michele doesn't log or dub tapes, she might handle correspondence from other companies. Or cast people needed for a show. Or return calls that her boss doesn't have time to deal with. Or take notes at a meeting. Or send faxes. Or photocopy reports. Does it sound as if Michele works hard? She does! Her day doesn't end when the clock strikes a certain hour. It ends when she's finished all her assignments.

On most days Michele is staked out at the main office, but "if they need an extra hand, they ask me to go on shoots." A **shoot** is a session of filming or videotaping. "On a shoot," says Michele, "a PA can get really lousy tasks or something fun. One time I had to hold water and a towel for a big TV star. Another time I drove around for two hours looking for a certain chicken cutlet that a rapper wanted." PAs on shoots can also be assigned to work on cue cards, get papers signed or move equipment. "Sometimes they even need you as an extra or someone in the audience," Michele says.

RELATED JOBS:
Runner
Production manager
Associate producer
Camera operator

Michele says that being a PA is tough. But she likes the fact that "it's active. It's never the same." She also says it's great to "meet a lot of people." But the best thing about being a PA is that you can learn about all aspects of TV. Production assistants do all different kinds of things. They see almost every side of TV production. PAs can learn how to use equipment. They can ask a lot of questions. And they can observe and absorb the way things work. By gaining skill, knowledge and experience, a PA gets ready for the step up to bigger things.

Have You Got What It Takes?

Production assistants work long hours. You have to be ready to do anything at any time. And you have to think of ways to get things done. But if you want to get into TV, PA work is an important step!

"A PA CAN GET REALLY LOUSY TASKS OR SOMETHING FUN."

Michele started her TV career as an **intern.** "MTV was coming to shoot a comedy show at my school," she explains. "A woman was posting a notice that said that they needed interns to help when they taped. So I called, and she said I could do it.

"For the next two days I interned for MTV. I made sure I was approachable." Michele says that it's important to show your willingness to do things. "If you cringe in the corner, they won't ask you to do things. But if you show enthusiasm, they'll give you more responsibility." Michele's enthusiasm paid off. The network brought her on as a regular intern. A few months later, a producer hired her as a PA.

PAs are near the bottom of the ladder, and sometimes that's a tough place to be. You have to take a lot of orders without feeling upset or kicked around. And sometimes you have to deal with frustrated producers and crew members. So production assistants need to be able to take things in stride. You can't let a bad day get you down.

A PA at work on the set.

And a PA has to be ready for a change at any moment. Michele has learned this through experience. "I was working on a daily show," she remembers, "and was under a serious deadline. Then we had a staff meeting and *boom*, the show was canceled."

This happens a lot in TV. Jobs are **free-lance** and rarely long-term. A crew works as long as a project lasts and then finds a new project to work on. Trying to get the next job takes time and energy. Luckily, Michele was hired to work on another show.

If you want to be a PA, try to get an interview or a trial day of work. Keep your eyes and ears open for anyone who can help you meet the right person in TV. You can also look up production companies in the phone book. Call them and offer your services for free.

To build some skills while you're waiting to get your foot in the door, take classes. Courses in photography, sound, lighting, communications or TV will come in handy. Volunteer to work backstage in your school or local theater production. Typing and word processing skills are helpful too, so work on those if you can.

Another smart move is to learn how to use a home video camera. Anybody can work one. And the camcorder you get at the corner electronics store is not that different from the one the pros use.

Since home video recorders are pretty expensive, you might want to borrow the equipment from your school or someone you know who has it. Electronics dealers also rent equipment. Look under "video dealer" and "video rental" in your yellow pages.

Once you get your hands on a camera, shoot everything in sight. See what works and what doesn't. Find out what looks good and what looks terrible. Let yourself make lots of mistakes—you can always tape over them. Using a camera will give you some experience before you even have a job.

GRIP

Nuts and Bolts of the Job

It's the most exciting scene on the show yet. The hero is stuck on the top of an unfinished skyscraper. He's clinging to a wooden beam, wondering how he's going to escape the gunman who's chasing him. Everything seems so real, but this is a TV show. It's on *film*. Who figured out how to get cameras up there? And who *put* those cameras up there?

J.D. did. He's a grip. It's his job to rig lights and cameras wherever they need to be, no matter where that is.

A TV crew usually has three or four grips. The **key grip** is the grip in charge. Grips work closely with the electricians so that the cameras and lights will have power. The head electrician is called the **gaffer**. Grips and gaffers are also responsible for safety on the set.

Grips need to be mechanical engineers, trapeze artists and brave soldiers all at once. They often have to rig cameras and lights in tricky places: an unfinished building, a tree or a roller coaster. A director or a producer tells a grip what lighting or camera effect he or she wants. "But they never tell you how to do it," says J.D. "It's your job to figure out how."

When cameras need mobility, J.D. has a couple of options. He can mount the camera on a **dolly,** which "looks like a platform on a railroad track." A dolly has wheels and moves the camera smoothly. J.D. can also get together with the carpenter and build a ramp. Basically, he'll do anything to get the camera from point A to point B the way the director wants it.

As for lights, grips work to create the right brightness and shadow. To create the right light effect, J.D. might use barn doors. Barn doors are metal flaps that are attached on four sides to movie lights. They can be tilted at different angles to control the light. J.D. also uses flags, which are like little movie screens on stands. "You use a flag to take light off where it's not wanted." Bounce cards are white, shiny cards that reflect light where it *is* wanted.

Grips are constantly climbing into odd and scary places to fasten a light source or camera to the perfect spot. If there's no perfect place to attach the light or camera, J.D. and the crew will build a scaffold to hold it.

RELATED JOBS:
Key grip
Gaffer
Best boy
Prop master

On the day of a shoot, J.D. gets up around 6:30 A.M. and goes to the set or location where they're going to shoot. Then he loads in. Loading in is getting all of the equipment out of the truck and onto the set. It usually takes about an hour.

When the equipment is loaded in, the lighting director meets with the key grip and the gaffer and tells them how he wants things set up. Then the key grip and the gaffer come up with a game plan to make it happen. They often use a one-and-one system, which means that one grip and one electrician work together on a project. As the day goes on, the key grip and the gaffer check with the lighting director for more instructions.

"I LIKE HEIGHTS. THEY ADD THAT BIT OF EXCITEMENT."

A grip rigs lights wherever they need to be!

When the shooting is over, J.D. has more work to do. "At the end of the day you have to break down everything you put together and leave the place just as it was when you came in." By the time J.D. gets into his truck to go home, he's usually put in 14 to 16 hours.

J.D. loves being a grip. And he's got the right personality for it too. "I like heights," he says. "They add that bit of excitement. I've been hanging off the side of a cliff or at the top of an unfinished skyscraper with just the rails and the I-beams in place." There's no doubt about it. Gripping is adventurous!

Have You Got What It Takes?

Being a grip is exciting. But it's also pretty tricky. You have to figure out ways to rig lights and cameras in strange places. Then you have to rig them! You have to work long hours. And it's a lot of manual labor. Think you can handle it? J.D can!

"I knew I liked working with my hands," J.D. says. "But after high school I floated around doing different jobs. I was the line operator for a cable company, and I worked in a liquor store. When I was 22 or so, a friend who worked at a local studio asked if I was interested in a job there." The job was production assistant, and J.D. took it. He says that while he was working as a PA, "I just kept my eyes and ears open. There was so much to learn. I became friends with grips, prop masters and electricians."

When J.D. decided to become a grip, he got into the **union** through the studio where he was working as a PA. Since then he's been getting grip jobs. He hears about most of these jobs from grips and other people in TV.

J.D. says that to be a grip you've got to be able to work well with people. "You're under the gun to get the job done," he explains. "If you can't get people to work with you, you end up doing it all by yourself. Then it takes too long." It's important to work together to set up those lights and cameras. Also, you're around the rest of the grip crew all day, so it's important that you get along.

J.D. adds, "It's a lot of manual labor. There are days when I feel like I'm just hired from the neck down. They just need sheer manpower." It might take ten minutes to think of a brilliant plan for rigging a light. But it might take three hours to make that brilliant plan happen. Grip work can be backbreakingly tough. And not every day holds thrills and excitement.

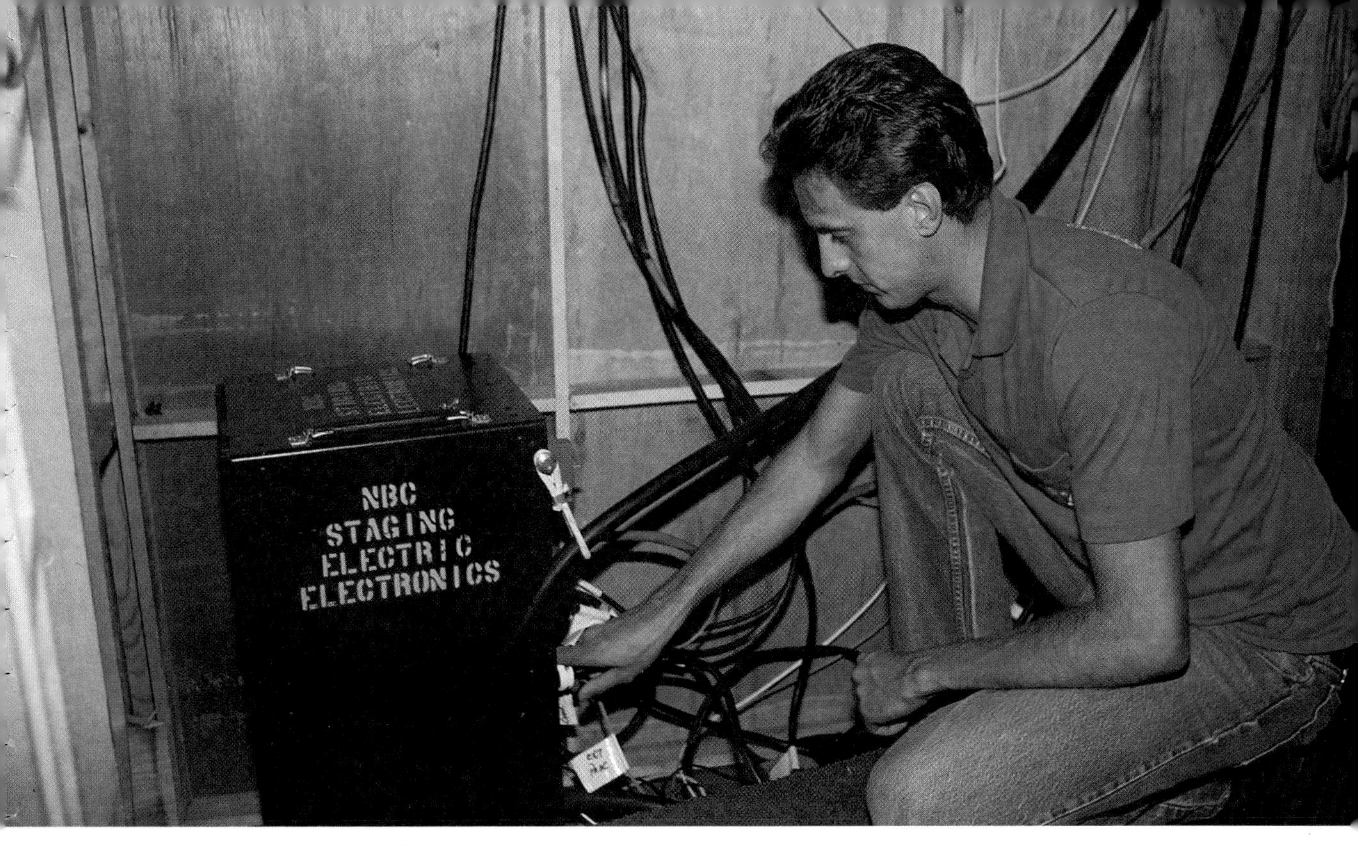

A grip needs to have a basic understanding of electricity.

If you want to be a grip, shop class is a must. It is also helpful to know about electricity and wiring. So read some books about electricity or talk to someone you know who's handy.

School and local stage productions require special lighting. And even though lighting for theater is different from lighting for cameras, it will help you get familiar with lights. So join the crew whenever you can.

You can also practice different kinds of camera movement with a home video camera. Try rigging it to a skateboard or a pulley and see what effects you can achieve. It's great practice!

CAMERA OPERATOR

Nuts and Bolts of the Job

You're watching a news program and the reporter is interviewing a guy on an archeological dig. He has just found another dinosaur skeleton and has a new theory about evolution. But he's standing in the middle of a desert. There's nothing anywhere around. Who goes to these strange places to film people like this? Who gets the action on film?

Camera operators like John do. John handles the camera on a shoot. He also works with the producer to come up with ideas about how to film shows and interviews.

Most of John's work is out of the studio and **on location.** He goes with a sound engineer and a producer on shoots. The producer usually has a general idea of what the audience should see. John adds to the producer's ideas. He makes sure that the producer will have all the images he or she needs to tell a story.

John also takes care of the technical side of things. He decides where to put the camera. And he makes decisions about the lighting exposure, the focus, and the width of the shot. "I'm director of photography and lighting, and key grip all at once," he says.

"I get to work in a lot of natural situations," John says. That means he's often capturing real life as it happens. Natural situations are exciting. But sometimes they're difficult to shoot. You can't exactly yell, "Cut!" in the middle of a boxing match just because you didn't get the right camera angle!

"I go into a situation, look at it and see how I'm going to handle it," John explains. He always tries to get the best shot. "Since I'm not in a studio, there are limits to what I can do. I try to figure out what's in my bag of tricks that will help." "Bag of tricks" really means "car full of stuff" that John takes wherever he goes. He's got lots of lights and reflective panels to bounce and control the light. He also has **filters.**

Sometimes John uses fog "to give the room more depth. It creates shafts of light and softens the image." And finally, John has got a **camrail.** That's a small track that lets the camera move smoothly within a 10-foot area. "A little motion adds so much," says John.

John can see exactly how his shot looks by checking his **monitor**—a TV-like screen that shows exactly what the camera sees. The monitor also lets the producer keep tabs on the camera work. Every now and then John plays back something he just videotaped to make sure it's what the producer wants.

RELATED JOBS:
Camera operator for a large studio
Grip

Aside from getting the best possible shot, John has to think about what the next picture in the story is going to be. He likes to use **B-roll** or **cutaway.** You see a cutaway when different images are shown on screen while a person is talking in the background. Say someone is interviewing a boxer who's talking about how hard he trained. Instead of looking at his face while he talks, you might see him jabbing at a punching bag. Or you might see the stadium where he's going to fight. That's a cutaway. Cutaways keep a story interesting because they pack more into each moment.

Every day as a camera operator is different. "I could be on skid

A camera operator at work on the set of a talk show.

row shooting a documentary, or I could be out in the orange groves profiling a farmer for an orange juice company," John says. He has to be ready to head out on a day's notice. And he often has to work on weekends, holidays or late at night.

On an average day, "I get up early and pack up my equipment. I double-check to make sure I have everything and that everything is working. Then I head out to the location." On location, John hooks up with the producer and finds out what the producer wants to shoot. Together they come up with a game plan. After that, John sets up.

John takes about an hour to set up his lights and cameras. Then he videotapes everything he needs at that location, and everyone moves on to the next place. "Sometimes we cover five to ten locations in a day," he says. When the producer has enough footage to make a good story, everyone packs up and goes home. John's usually out on location for 10 to 12 hours at a time.

In spite of the long hours, John loves being a camera operator. He says it's great because of "all the different situations and events I get to see and all the different people I meet." The camera operator usually gets to show up for the most exciting part of the process: the action. The interview with the crime boss. The rock concert. The archeological dig. John doesn't have to do much preshoot planning. He goes in, talks to the producer, gets the footage, and hands the tape to the producer.

Have You Got What It Takes?

Even though John films a lot of exciting events, being a camera operator isn't all fun and games. You have to be ready and able to go to any kind of shoot when you're needed. You have to manage a lot of camera and video equipment. And you have to work in situations that you can't control. But if you're like John, being a camera operator is the job for you!

John set his sights on becoming a camera operator when he was in high school. "I didn't go to college. Instead I hustled my way into a local PBS station as a runner," he says. "I did errands and biked film back and forth."

John knew that he could learn a lot as a runner. He "got to see a

"I GET TO WORK IN A LOT OF NATURAL SITUATIONS."

little from every department." And he took advantage of his learning position. He even joined a crew as a sound assistant just to watch a good camera operator in action! Eventually he gained enough experience to be the camera operator in a local studio. Now he runs his own production company.

A camera operator needs to have a good eye. As John puts it, "You need a good visual sense." That means knowing what will look great on film. To gain that skill, you should learn about photography. "Photography is the basis of the whole thing. You should never try operating a video camera unless you've had some time with a still camera." Photography classes are a good place to start. Or you can learn by taking pictures. You need to understand some principles of light and composition.

John started fiddling with a camera when he was in junior high school. "I took stills with my friends all the time," he says. After junior high, John went to a vocational high school, where he learned about video equipment.

Being a camera operator requires some skill with a home video camera. You can practice holding the camera perfectly steady or moving it smoothly and cleanly. Neither technique is easy. Videotape people sitting and talking to you. And shoot action stuff. Work on keeping your subject in sharp focus. All of these things will teach you a lot. Before you know it, you may be a camera operator like John.

"PHOTOGRAPHY IS THE BASIS OF THE WHOLE THING."

SOUND ENGINEER

Nuts and Bolts of the Job

You're watching your favorite talk show when suddenly an argument breaks out between one of the guests and a person in the audience. They're practically screaming at each other. But somehow you can hear exactly what each of them is saying. Is it magic?

No. It's a good sound engineer. And his name is Jorge. Jorge is the sound engineer for two different talk shows. He manages a group of people called the audio crew. The audio crew handles all the sounds on a TV show. Those sounds include every word and noise that you hear.

"The business of sound can get very complicated," says Jorge. Have you ever seen a news show where several reporters in different places can talk to and hear each other? Jorge oversees this kind of communication on his shows. He makes sure that the shows' crew members can communicate among themselves. And he has to make sure that the studio audience can hear what's happening.

Jorge and his crew are responsible for getting the sounds to the viewer in the clearest way possible. "If someone has to say, 'What did they say?' or 'What was that?' we didn't do our job right," he says.

During taping, Jorge sits in a room in the back of the studio. He surrounds himself with monitors that show what each camera sees. "The more I can see, the better," says Jorge.

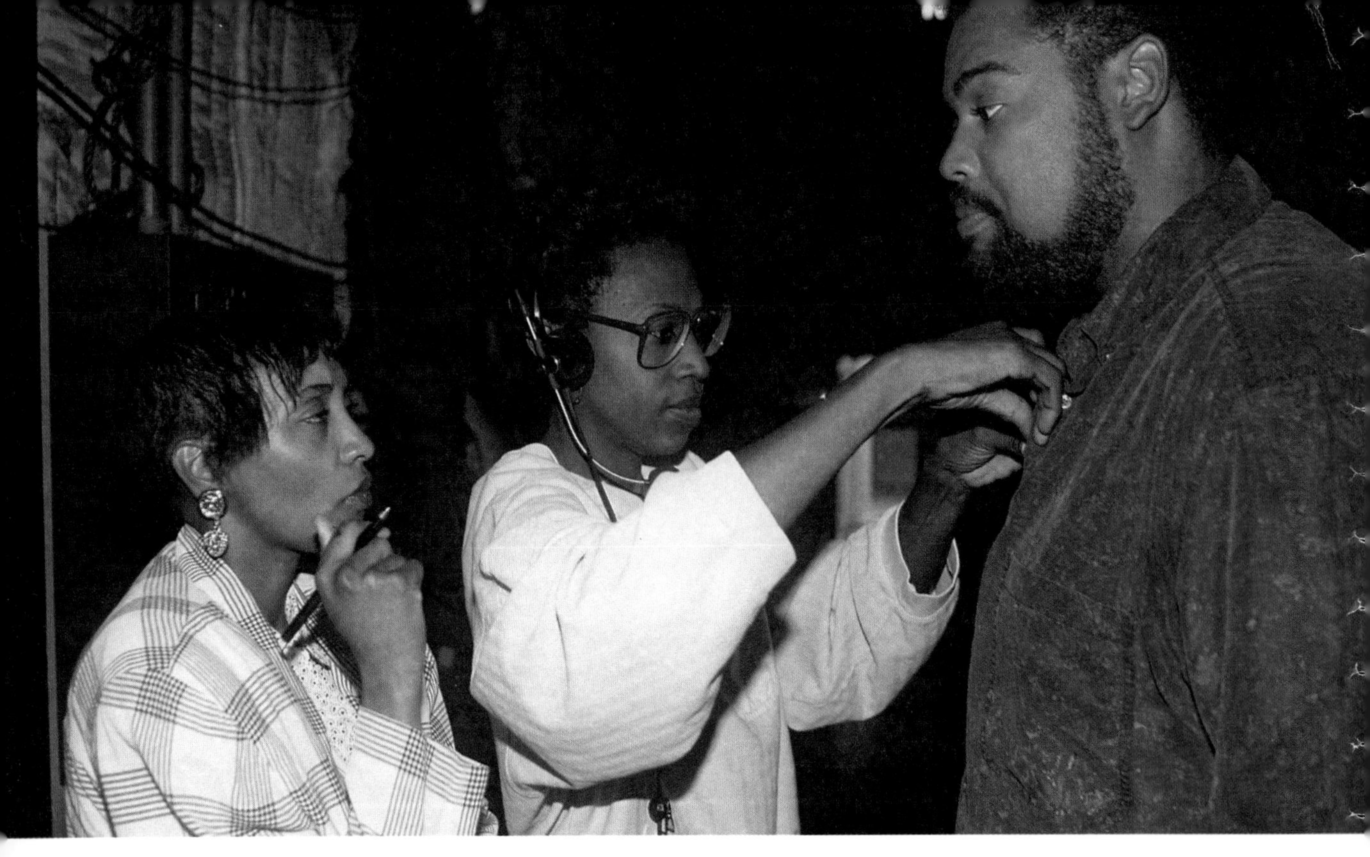

An audio technician checks an actor's microphone.

"I sit in front of a huge **mixing board** with lots of dials and buttons," Jorge explains. He uses a mixing board to balance all the sounds. The sounds can include the host talking, the guests talking and the audience talking. They can also include people standing by outside the studio or music coming in and out of commercials.

All the sounds come in at different volumes and from different places. Jorge has a lot to handle when he's balancing sounds. He says it's like "filling a glass of water. You can only put so much sound in at one time. I try to keep the glass as full as possible without spilling." If there's too much sound, it will start to sound unpleasant. So Jorge works to deliver smooth, clear sounds.

Jorge's call time, the official arrival time, is usually early in the morning. "We get about an hour for **engineering setup,** or ESU," he says. "Then we're in production. Sometimes we tape two or three shows a day with a break in between."

When the tapings are over, Jorge takes care of postproduction tasks. He might have to tape a voiceover. A voiceover is a segment or commercial in which someone you can't see explains what's being shown on the screen. Jorge might also have to do a promotion for the next day's show. When he's finished, Jorge can go home—or start over at his other talk show!

RELATED JOBS:
Engineering assistant
Boom operator
Sound effects editor

Even though his work is tough, Jorge gets a thrill from the challenges of being a sound engineer. "I like to walk into a studio and in the least amount of time figure my way through the sound system," he says. "I work for the satisfaction of doing a show without mistakes," he says.

Have You Got What It Takes?

Being a sound engineer is complicated. You have to manage a crew of people. You have to watch several monitors at once. And you have to balance the sounds just right. That's a lot. But it's not too much for Jorge!

Jorge came to New York to study recording—making a tape or disc in a studio. He learned a lot from watching recording engineers work. "I was an assistant to the recording engineers and developed these skills," he says. Since Jorge's bosses also owned a

"THE BUSINESS OF SOUND CAN GET VERY COMPLICATED."

A sound engineer makes sure that the audience hears exactly what is being said on the show.

film company, Jorge could try his hand at film sound. "I have always enjoyed the idea of sound with picture," says Jorge dreamily. "I fell in love with that."

After working in film for a while, Jorge wandered into TV. He's worked in TV for the past nine years. He says he likes it "because of the immediacy." You work on it, then you see and hear it on the air very soon.

A sound engineer should be good at working with machines. Jorge says it's also good if you're fast-thinking and able to adapt to anything. And of course it helps if you love sound. That means all sound—music, crunching snow, shouting—everything. Jorge says that a typical sound engineer is "someone who fusses with the stereo dials until the music is perfect."

"I WORK FOR THE SATISFACTION OF DOING A SHOW WITHOUT MISTAKES."

If you want to be a sound engineer, you should start by becoming aware of sounds—especially sounds that are created or recorded. Listen to everything, from classical music to TV dialogue to sound effects. It all gets recorded and brought to your ears by people like Jorge.

There aren't really classes in sound engineering. But you can volunteer to work the sound board at a club where bands play. Local and school theaters need crew members to work with sound too. So get out there and see what you can do with sound. You may become a pro like Jorge.

HAIRSTYLIST

Nuts and Bolts of the Job

When you turn on your favorite TV show, you see familiar characters. You watch them all the time. You know what they look like and how they act. And you'd know in a second if one of them changed his or her hair. Hair is a big part of each character's personality.

Who's responsible for an actor's hair? Who comes up with all those styles that look great on camera?

Pauletta does. Pauletta styles hair for a major comedy-variety show. She's in charge of all the actors' hairstyles on the show.

Hairstylists do more than fix hair. They help create characters. Do you think someone with every strand in place will have the same personality as a character whose hair is all over the place? Probably not. Hairstylists like Pauletta have to come up with looks that fit each character's personality. The hairstyles also have to work with the director's vision of the show as a whole. Aside from that, hairstylists use hairdos to re-create time periods, reflect social class, or fudge a character's age.

Pauletta prepares for a day on the set by reading the **script.** A script is a copy of the text used in theater, film, radio, or TV. "I take the script and figure out everything that pertains to hair," she says. If Pauletta is doing hair for a skit in which an actor is imitating a real person, she needs to copy the real person's hair. She might even exaggerate it to make the imitiation funnier.

If Pauletta is doing hair for a new character, she works with the actor and gets an idea of how he or she wants to look. Pauletta also teams up with the makeup artist. "Sometimes she'll have an idea, and we'll go through a few possibilities until we decide what to do. I also work with a **prosthetics** person." He or she handles the fake noses, foreheads and chins "that make actors look like other people," Pauletta explains.

When the show is being taped, Pauletta is usually in the dressing room cranking out all these looks she's helped invent. Or she might be hopping around the set with her trusty set bag. A set bag is a minisuit-case. It contains things like rubber bands, water, hair spray, bobby pins, and spirit gum. Spirit gum is a glue for attaching prosthetics to the skin. The set bag has whatever Pauletta needs to prepare characters.

RELATED JOBS:
Makeup artist
Special effects makeup artist
Assistant hairstylist

Pauletta works long days when the show is being taped. She has to be at work by 7:45 A.M., when the show's dancers come in to get their hair and makeup done. Taping the dance routines starts at

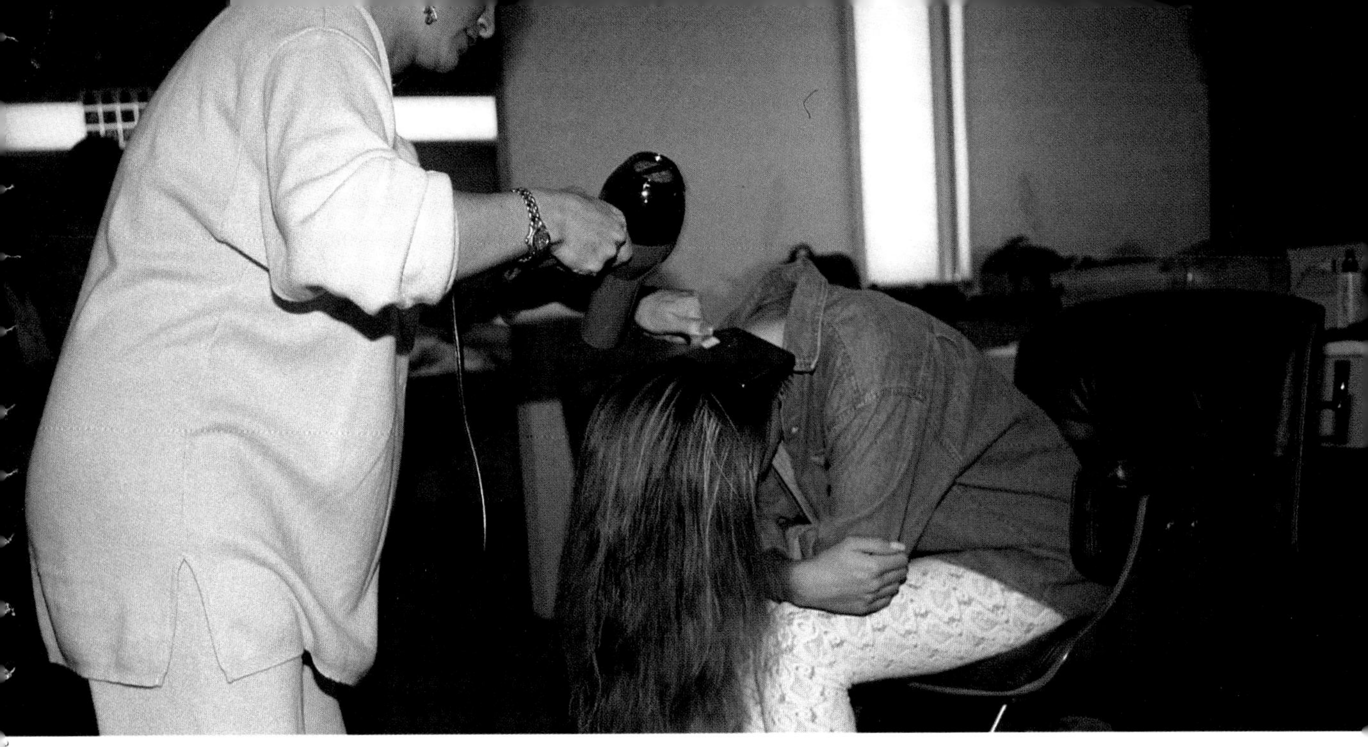

On the set, a hairstylist must work quickly.

10:00 and usually lasts for a couple of hours. "In between numbers we only have 20 minutes to change 5 women—that's hair, makeup and wardrobe. There's not a second to waste." Now that's high-pressure hairstyling!

After a lunch break, rehearsal begins for the rest of the show. Even when it's just a rehearsal, Pauletta does the hair for each skit. She likes the practice. It also helps the actors get used to their costumes and styling.

After a dinner break the real taping begins. While the audience assembles, Pauletta prepares the actors who are in the first skit. While the actors perform, Pauletta's assistants stand backstage to keep an eye on their hair. But, she says, "If it's something really difficult, like wigs, I'll be up there myself."

While the first skit is being taped, Pauletta is usually backstage getting other actors ready for the next skit. "It takes a lot of patience," Pauletta explains, "because there can be lots of takes of each skit." They'll do it over and over until the director is happy. Some days of taping last until 2:00 A.M.!

Even though days on the set can be long, Pauletta loves doing hair. She's been at it for 21 years. She says that her favorite part of the job is creating characters. She also loves being able to do all different kinds of things with hair. "You get to do a lot of things—old-fashioned stuff, everything imaginable. You get to show what you can do. Every week there's a different challenge." Since hairstyles are always changing, the job never gets boring. There's always something new to try.

Have You Got What It Takes?

Pauletta is crazy about her job. But she does admit that it's a lot of work. "People think it's glamour and glitz, but we work very long hours. If you don't like to work, don't get into this business." Aside from the long hours, you have to have a lot of patience. You have to be creative. And you have to come through in a pinch. Think you can handle it?

Pauletta has always been a hard worker. She went to high school and **cosmetology school** at the same time. "I had a lot of homework," remembers Pauletta. But she earned her diploma and her cosmetology license in one fell swoop.

"Then I got my first job at $47 a week," she remembers. "I was so happy to get that. It was a wig shop and beauty salon." Pauletta worked in salons for several years. The rest, she says, "is a

"I FIGURE OUT EVERYTHING THAT PERTAINS TO HAIR IN THE SCRIPT."

Cinderella story." She was working in a salon and a show needed a hairstylist. Someone recommended Pauletta, and she never went back to the beauty shop again. She became a TV hairstylist for good.

To be a TV hairstylist, you need a lot of patience. Those hairdos have to look great for every single take! Pauletta says you also "have to be versatile" and that you "have to learn all types of hair." Plus, you have to be creative enough to come up with new styles.

If you want to be a hairstylist, you can practice your craft on your own tresses. Work on your friends' hair, too. Do girl's hair and guy's hair. Build up a range of looks you can do. Check out hairstyles around town. And check out hairstyles on TV and in movies. You can also offer to do hair in school or local stage productions.

During taping, a hairstylist might work with dozens of actors!

Before you can work with hair for a living, you need a license. For that, you can go to beauty or cosmetology school. There are lots of good beauty schools around. But some so-called beauty schools don't provide the training they promise. So it's a good idea to check with the Better Business Bureau before you enroll.

COSTUME DESIGNER

Nuts and Bolts of the Job

The dramatic music from your television set fills the room. The annual Christmas ball in Rome Valley is in full swing. The townspeople are decked out in their finest clothes. Sparkling gowns glimmer, and bright fabrics catch your eye. They look even better than last year.

Who makes scenes like this one come alive? Who plans all those great outfits?

It's the job of costume designer Maggie. Maggie works for a daily network soap opera. She decides what people on the show will wear.

Maggie takes the director's vision of each soap opera episode and applies it to the clothes. The director may want to show a certain time period, mood, or set of colors. It's Maggie's job to make that time period, mood, or set of colors really come through in the characters' clothing.

Maggie also uses clothes to help establish the characters on the show. Clothes are a reflection of personality. By overseeing the wardrobe, Maggie contributes to the development of the characters. "For example," she says, "we have an actress who plays twins, so I have to use their costumes to help set them apart. One is bad and sexy, the other is good and soft-spoken."

One of the most important tools for Maggie and the rest of the costume staff is the **breakdown.** A breakdown is a summary of an upcoming episode. It describes each scene. It tells Maggie which actors are appearing, where the scenes take place and what weather goes with the story line. All this information helps Maggie make decisions about costumes. It tells her things like which sets she has to match and whether the actors will need to wear raincoats.

Once Maggie has read the breakdown, she and her staff can forge ahead with costumes. They pull costumes from the show's wardrobe. Wardrobe is a show's collection of costumes. "Each character has his or her own closet of clothes that fit the character." Maggie tries to use these clothes for each episode. If wardrobe doesn't have the right outfit, Maggie will shop for it.

Some episodes require special costume planning. A character might go from rich to poor and need new clothes. Or there might be a theme party where everybody in the cast has to dress alike. Or maybe a new character is coming on the show. These are all things that Maggie needs to know about. So Maggie has regular meetings with the producers of the show to find out what's coming up.

Maggie must plan dozens and dozens of costumes. And she has many things to think about. "I consider silhouette, color, and

"I CONSIDER SILHOUETTE, COLOR, AND PEOPLE'S BODIES."

people's bodies," she says. She also has to think about the set designs, lighting, makeup, and hairstyles in creating her looks. There's a lot of stuff to match, a million elements to juggle.

While all costume designers deal with costumes, the job varies depending on what kind of show or movie you're working on. Since Maggie works for an hour-long show that's aired five days a week, she handles a lot of volume.

RELATED JOBS:
Wardrobe handler
Stylist
Costume assistant

Maggie also handles a grueling schedule. Her day starts at 7:00 A.M. and finishes at 7:00 P.M.—if everything goes perfectly. If there are any problems or delays, Maggie's day can last until late into the night.

Sometimes Maggie and the rest of the cast and crew go on location. They leave the studio to shoot scenes in a special place. "Being on location can be crazy," says Maggie. She remembers one time in particular. "We were shooting a Cinderella wedding in a park in Manhattan," she tells us. "One actress was supposed to waltz with her prince. But it had been raining and the ground was wet. Before long, her entire gown was covered in mud. The crew and I rescued the dress with towels, a water spritzer and a blow-dryer."

Besides the hours she spends on the set and on location, Maggie does other costume work for the show. She goes wardrobe shopping "at least once a week." She meets with actors who need fittings. And she "gets together with the wardrobe staff and pulls clothes for upcoming shows."

During tapings, Maggie watches the actors on a TV monitor to see how the costumes will look to the viewers. Once in a while something doesn't come across well. It might be that a shade of red doesn't look good on a certain actor. Or that two outfits in the same scene don't look good on camera together. Or that a bra strap is showing. Such things are Maggie's responsibility. Her staff takes care of smaller problems like broken belt buckles or lost buttons.

Maggie really loves her job. She says that it's great because "it's exciting—never the same." She is especially proud of the parties. "The big extravaganzas—they've been right on the money," she says. Maggie regularly coordinates a ballroom full of characters in designer wear. And each costume has to look fantastic on camera and fit each character's personality. That takes a lot of creativity and coordination.

A costume designer coordinates the wardrobe for a show.

Have You Got What It Takes?

You have to consider a lot when you're planning the costumes for a ballroom scene on a soap opera. You have to think of the set, the characters, and the scene. You have to make sure that every detail looks just right. And you have to be able to fix things in a pinch. It's a lot to handle!

Maggie learned most of her craft from experience. When she moved to New York, she was ready to take any costume-related work she could find. And she did. "I worked in a costume shop. I worked in a hat shop. I did clothes for off-off-off-Broadway projects," she tells us. "I made jewelry and hats for Broadway shows." All these jobs helped Maggie "learn a lot about how costumes are put together, how to find clothes and where to buy things." And all of those tasks are important!

Maggie's hands-on costume experience helped her build her **portfolio.** A costume designer's portfolio is a book with pictures of all the costumes the designer has created. It also has pictures of costumes he or she would like to create in the future.

Maggie's portfolio got her an assistant designer job. After that she was a free-lance costume designer and stylist for several years. Now she works in daytime drama.

A costume designer needs to be creative. Maggie says that she "was always very good at arts and crafts." You should also be insightful about people and personalities. And you should have an eye for color and composition. A good sense of style helps too. And if you love to shop, that's a plus.

If you want to be a costume designer, it's a good idea to take classes in fashion or costume design. Classes in figure drawing, color theory, costume history, and sewing will all be helpful too.

Maggie recommends any kind of clothes-making or even clothes-selling job to get you going. She also suggests that you "assist in small projects," like your local community theater. Try to meet people who work in the business. Even shopping can be good experience. "It helps make you aware of what's going on in fashion," she says. Just be sure to leave your wallet at home so you don't spend a fortune!

Nuts and Bolts of the Job

You love to watch this on-screen character. Sure, the actor is good-looking. But it's more than that. You can relate to the character himself. You know what he's going through. You understand how he's feeling. That's because the actor who plays him in very good at his craft. Who is he?

He's Tom. Tom is an actor who gets most of his acting jobs from TV commercials. He also performs on stage and in film.

These days, both men and women call themselves "actors." An actor takes a make-believe character and gives that character life. Actors learn about the characters they play from scripts.

"THERE'S ALWAYS THE POSSIBILITY OF GETTING THAT BIG BREAK."

A good actor makes you forget that he or she is a regular person. When you watch a good actor perform, you get caught up in the character and his or her story. You even forget that the actor really isn't the character being played.

An actor uses instinct, imagination, and past experiences to figure out what the character would do at any given moment. What would the expression on Juliet's face be when she first sees Romeo? Does the neighborhood bully shout his threats or hiss them quietly? An actor is constantly making decisions about his or her character. That's why no two characters or performances are the same.

A person who plans to make a movie, TV show, or commercial sends out a breakdown. A breakdown is a summary of the story line. It's similar to the breakdown that Maggie, the costume designer, works with, but it also includes a list of the different people needed to be cast for the project. A cast list might say, "One handsome but slightly dangerous teenage boy. A Luke Perry type. One quiet, bookworm-type girl to play his younger sister." Several breakdowns get published in a giant memo that is sent to agents and managers.

Agents look at breakdowns every day and decide which of their actors might be right for the parts. If an agent has an actor who fits the description on a cast list, the agent will send head shots to the appropriate casting directors. A headshot is a glossy 8″ × 10″ photo of the actor. A casting director matches up actors to projects. The casting directors look over the head shots and call the actors they want to audition.

RELATED JOBS:
Voiceover person
TV or movie extra

When Tom arrives at an audition, he signs in. Then someone takes a Polaroid picture of him so the casting director can remember what he looks like. After that, the person in charge of the waiting room usually gives Tom some

Some actors send out two types of head shots—a happy look for commercial work and a more serious look for film work.

copy. Copy is the lines that an actor has to say in the commercial.

Then Tom will sit down and go over the copy. He tries to make it stick in his mind. But, he says, "You don't try to memorize—repeat, do *not* try to memorize" the lines. This is because there are cue cards at auditions. And the important part is getting "the gist—the basic structure—of the story. Otherwise you're just reading," Tom says.

When the casting director calls Tom's name, he goes into a room with "a video camera and a couple of lights and a cue card." There might also be a table, a chair or the product being advertised. A casting director usually lets the actors do a practice run if they want to. "Some actors get their best performance after a practice run," Tom says. "But I don't do that because I've already played it out in my mind and I'm ready to go."

After Tom performs his part in the commercial once, the casting director will usually ask him to do it again. Tom might be asked to make the character more of a jock or to play the character younger. The second try doesn't mean that Tom did a bad job the first time. The casting director just wants to test all the possibilities and see the range of characters that Tom can handle well.

Tom always leaves as soon as the audition is over. "It's bad to stay and chat with the casting director, even if it's someone you know, Tom explains. "You want your performance to be the last thing that sticks in the casting director's mind. I like to hit 'em hard and then leave."

In some commercials there's no talking, just things happening. To audition for these kinds of commercials, the casting director will ask Tom to **improvise** a situation. "For example," Tom explains, "I'll be told, 'You're making a pizza and everything goes wrong.'" So Tom has to go up there and create an invisible kitchen and a problem pizza. "The creativity comes from thinking of what no other actor would think of," Tom says. "I'm gonna make that kitchen catch on fire and have the pizza stick to the ceiling. Total chaos."

If he's lucky, Tom's creativity wins him a callback. A **callback** is another audition. When you're called back, it means you're still being considered for a commercial. If Tom doesn't get a callback, he hopes the casting director will at least remember him for the future.

Tom doesn't get booked, or cast in, a commercial very often. There are many actors out there and not very many jobs. The odds are tough. To get one job out of every 20 auditions is considered great. Many actors audition for years and never book a job at all.

Acting in commercials is not as glamorous as you might think. "You have to stand around for hours and hours while the crew takes care of the sets and the sound and the technical stuff. Even if you've got a major part," Tom says, "you spend only a tiny portion of the day actually performing. Maybe an hour. But you have to be ready to go at any moment." Whew!

Tom might have some dry spells with no auditions, but it's normal for him to go on one or two auditions a day—usually for commercials. His agent tells him a day or so before the commercial what he's trying out for. "I try to dress to fit the type they're after. If I need to look like a kid, I wear a neon shirt and high-tops."

At 3:00 P.M. Tom goes to his second job. He works at a fancy hotel as a porter. Most actors have two jobs. "Out of all the actors in this country," Tom explains, "only 10 percent make more than $3,000 per year at their craft." Actors tend to work at jobs that give them time off during the day for auditions.

Even though it's tough being an actor, Tom says that it's definitely worth it. The best part is "booking a job. It makes you feel good that you chose to be an actor. It means 'Yes, you're needed. You're good.'" And there's always the possibility of getting that big break, becoming famous and getting great roles that show off your talent.

Have You Got What It Takes?

An actor goes on countless auditions. You have to come up with new ways to play characters. And you probably have to work a second job to help pay the rent. But Tom says that being an actor is definitely worth it.

"ACTORS HIT A LOT OF OBSTACLES, EVEN IF THEY'RE TALENTED."

Sometimes an actor is prompted by cue cards off stage.

Tom dropped out of college when he came to New York City to go to acting school. After that, Tom and some friends rented a theater space with their own money and put on a play. "We sent out fliers to agents." Tom was fortunate enough to be asked to sign up with one of those agents. "It's not like it's been a breeze ever since," he says. "It just means I'm able to get auditions."

Tom says that for an actor, "the most important quality is persistence. Actors hit a lot of obstacles, even if they're talented. You hear the words 'No' and 'You didn't book it' all the time. But you have to put it in perspective and not take it personally."

If you want to be an actor, check out the performances of all the actors you see on TV and in movies. Who seems the most appealing and believable? What makes one actor different from the others? You can also audition for plays in your school or community. Take any part, even a tiny one. Or offer to work behind the scenes. That will give you the chance to watch more experienced actors in action. Also, Tom advises that you "get some formal training if you can. You'll use it your whole career."

When you think you're ready, have some headshots taken. Mail your headshots to lots of agencies. After that, "It's good to get into a play, any play," says Tom. "Join a local theater group or start one of your own. Then mail fliers to agents. It's proof that you're busy and committed. Good agents spend their free time looking for new talent. Just keep yourself visible."

FOUR THINGS TO REMEMBER NO MATTER WHAT TV JOB YOU WANT

1. Do your homework.

Find out what kinds of jobs are available. Use the library. If you're in school, ask your guidance counselor about internships or jobs in TV. He or she might know about programs that are right for you.

If you're in a small town, call the chamber of commerce and ask if there are any local TV stations. If you're near a major city, get in touch with the network branches or the local public TV station. You could also call or visit any nearby cable production companies. You can even look in the yellow pages under "television."

2. Get yourself out there.

Once you get in touch with these stations, ask if there are any entry-level positions. Ask what the qualifications are. If you're told there's nothing for you, ask if they're interested in taking an intern for free. No-cost labor can be hard to resist.

Next, get a résumé ready. A résumé should include (1) your name, address, and phone number, (2) your goal, (3) your level of schooling and the schools you went to, (4) your work experience, (5) your extra activities in school, like soccer team, film club, or makeup for the school plays, (6) any helpful skills, like typing, languages, computers, or mastery of home video equipment. A sample résumé can be found at the end of this chapter.

If you're mailing in a résumé, include a short letter telling why you're interested in working at the station. Let them know when you're available. Explain that you're really excited about any work the station might have.

If you go in for an interview, dress neatly. Answer all the questions you're asked as best you can. Be honest. Stress that you want to get experience and learn all you can. Don't be afraid to ask your interviewer a few questions too. You have to decide if the job seems fair and worth your time. Hopefully, you'll be offered a spot, you'll like the sound of it, and your TV career can begin.

Once you get an internship or a job, you already have your foot in the door. Now you need to work hard and learn as much as you can.

Be enthusiastic. Offer to help out whenever you can. Keep your eyes and ears open and watch how other people get their jobs done. And ask questions. Most people admire curiosity and are glad to help you out.

3. Find a mentor.

A mentor is someone who you can go to with questions, someone who will teach you what he or she knows. Usually a mentor is a person whom you help a lot too. And he or she takes extra time to explain things to you. A mentor might be someone you work with every day. Or it could be someone you work with only once in a while. The important thing is that you get to know that person. Watch your mentor work and ask questions. Tell your mentor what you'd like to do—he or she might be able to help you get there.

4. Work your way up.

Be prepared to work hard for little or no money in the beginning. The important thing is to get experience. That experience will help you get the job you want later.

Don't let a bad day get you down. Everybody has a bad day once in a while. If you feel a little discouraged, remember that you're not alone. Everyone has been where you are and has felt the way you do. The beginning of a career is always the hardest part. When things get tough, hang in there. Keep working toward your goal. You'll get there!

TV is an ever-growing industry with infinite possibilities. For every job we've described here, there are dozens more out there. And new kinds of TV jobs are invented every day. No two careers are the same. There are no rule books. So just jump in somewhere and see how it feels. Happy landings!

Eliot Smith
222 Eighth Avenue, #5C
Brooklyn, NY 11215
(718) 555-1234

Objective:

Internship or entry-level position in television production

Education:

John Jay High School, Brooklyn, NY
Class of 1994

Experience:

Shop assistant, Brighter Day Florwers, New York, NY. Part-time 9/91 to 6/93. Advised customers, operated cash register, built display structures, occasionally helped with bookkeeping.

Counselor, Park Slope YMCA Day Camp, Brooklyn, NY. Full-time 6/92 to 9/92. Supervised 10- through 12-year-old campers, taught soccer to all campers, drove van.

Other part-time jobs include shoveling walks, baby-sitting, and dog-walking for local residents.

Activities:

Junior varsity soccer team, 2 years
Varsity soccer team, 2 years (captain 1 year)
Varsity basketball team, 2 years
Spanish Club, 1 year
Key Club volunteer, 1 year

Skills:

Knowledge of home video equipment
Conversational Spanish
Basic carpentry
Ability to adapt to any situation

References are available upon request

GLOSSARY

actor A person who takes a character and gives that character life, as on television and in film. The character may be make-believe or based on a real person.

assistant hairstylist A person who assists the hairstylist.

associate producer A person who helps coordinate a show and make it run smoothly from day to day.

B-roll Extra footage that is shown while a person talks. It is used to highlight things the person says. Also known as a **cutaway.**

best boy The gaffer's assistant.

boom A long beam that's used to guide a microphone.

boom operator A person on the sound crew who controls the boom to record the most important sounds.

breakdown A description, scene by scene, of a script.

callback A second or third audition. Callbacks help narrow down the large number of actors who might audition for one part.

camera operator A person who operates a camera on a shoot. A camera operator makes decisions about lighting exposure, focus, and width of the shot.

camrail A 10-foot track the camera is attached to so it can move smoothly across a small space.

cosmetology school A beauty school that teaches hairstyling and/or makeup art.

costume assistant A person who assists the costume designer.

costume designer A person who decides what the actors on a television show will wear and then plans those outfits.

dolly A platform on a track used to move a camera during taping or filming.

engineering assistant A person who assists the sound engineer.

engineering setup (ESU) The time allowed for the sound crew to set up its equipment.

extra An actor who has no lines and appears in the background.

filter An attachment for the camera lens used to change the look or quality of the picture.

free-lance Being hired for and working on one project at a time instead of being a regular employee of a company.

gaffer The head electrician.

grip A person who sets up lights and cameras for television production.

hairstylist A person who styles actors' hair.

improvise To make something up as you go along. Actors are often asked to improvise scenes in an audition so that the director or casting director can see how creative he or she can be with a character.

intern A person who works for little or no pay for the experience of learning about the business.

key grip The head grip.

makeup artist A person who works to change an actor's appearance with makeup and prosthetics.

mixing board A large board with dials and levers that control the different sounds coming in. The sound engineer operates the mixing borad to balance all these sounds.

monitor A TV screen that shows the camera operator or producer exactly what the camera is recording.

on location A place where a show is taped or filmed away from the studio.

portfolio An artist's collection of his or her best work. A portfolio shows pictures of the costumes or makeup the designer or artist has created.

producer A person in charge of all or part of a show. The producer hires and supervises the crew on the show.

production assistant A person who handles simple production tasks on a television set.

production manager A person who organizes a shoot and handles the business end of it, such as paying bills.

prop master A person in charge of all the movable objects in a scene or on the set.

prosthetics Attachments, like fake noses, moustaches, or bald heads, used by the makeup crew to change a person's features.

runner A person with many of the same tasks as an intern, such as running errands or making photocopies. A runner is paid for the work and is a small step up from intern.

script The written text of a stage play, screenplay, or radio or television broadcast.

shoot A session of filming or videotaping.

sound effects editor A person who inserts the special noises that make a film or video sound realistic.

sound engineer A person who mixes sounds.

special effects makeup artist A makeup artist who helps the actor look as if something out of the ordinary has happened. For example, the makeup artist would create a face that's half skull or eyes that glow in the dark.

stylist A person who helps people on news or talk shows choose the clothes they will wear.

union A group of workers who join together to make sure they get fair pay and good working conditions.

voiceover person A person who comments or narrates off camera.

wardrobe handler An assistant to the costume designer who works directly with the clothing, doing the ironing, sewing, and mending.

INDEX